poems

by

PARADISE

FOR THE

PORTUGUESE

QUEEN

Benjamin

Ivry

Orchises Press

Washington

1998

Orchises Press
P.O. Box 20602
Alexandria, Virginia 22320-1602
G6E4C2A

I WOULD LIKE TO THANK FOR THEIR ENCOURAGEMENT:
Richard Howard, Dr. Martin Bax, Alice Quinn, Muriel Spark,
Penelope Jardine, Sidney Buckland, Carolyn Kizer, Renata
Gorczynski, Fernando Arrabal, Harold and Carol Rolfe,
Charity Hume, Martha Hollander, James Marrow, Emily
Rose, Simone Boué, Marie Ponsot, William Merwin, Claude
Lévi-Strauss, Mark Millkey, Peter McCurdy, Boonkhet
Hangsuwan, M.et Mme Gérard Worms, Jean-Michel
Hoppan, Prof. Billy Bussell Thompson, Ricardo Morin,
S. Abbas Raza, Hu Ying-Chieh, and Rogério de Souza Poly.

I can no longer personally thank the late and much regretted
James Ingram Merrill, E. M. Cioran, Gilles Deleuze and
Georges Duby.

Thanks are due to my publisher Roger Lathbury of Orchises
Press, and to the book's able designer, Jonathan Bumas.

Library of Congress Cataloging-in-Publication Data

Ivry, Benjamin
Paradise for the Portuguese queen:
poems /by Benjamin Ivry.
p. cm.
ISBN 0-914061-69-0
I. Title
PS3559. V53P37 1998
811'.54—dc 21   97-2538
CIP

Paradise

for the

Portuguese

Queen

for my family

Contents

Contents

ACKNOWLEDGEMENTS

These poems have previously appeared in periodicals:

AMBIT: *No Music; At the Jardins des Plantes Zoo; Edvard Munch to His Muse; Tapestry, Musée Marmottan; Funeral Music for Christian Dior; Failed Cathedrals; Cioran's Ideal Confessor, Judgment Day; Reading Proust in Barcelona; Birthplace of Colette; Poetry of Exile: Zagajewski and Brodsky; A Friend of Larkin's; From a Memoir of Auden; Longevity; Author Portrait; Tanka: Distractions of a Travelling Shot*

CHELSEA MAGAZINE: *Aquarium; A Lost Sugarcube Will Pursue You in Hell*

CQ: *Gerbrandt Van der Eeckhout's "Portrait of His Father"*

THE DENVER QUARTERLY: *A Prayer Against Strauss' "Salomé"; Rimbaud's Piano*

GREEN MOUNTAINS REVIEW: *Old Tenants*

THE LONDON REVIEW OF BOOKS: *Paradise for the Portuguese Queen*

THE NEW REPUBLIC: *Captions to Certain Slide Lectures; What Time Does a Chinaman Go to the Dentist?*

THE NEW YORKER: *Wet Autumn Night; Stained Glass at Père-Lachaise*

THE RIALTO: *Ten Lines Before the Mast*

THE SPECTATOR: *Meditation at a Bar; Skyscraper Dissuasion*

Apology to Saint Cecilia was published in a preface to "The Trouble with Being Born," by E.M. Cioran (Quartet Books, 1993)

The Bay of Rio appeared separately as an artist's book, with etchings by Jean Miotte (Keeser Editions, 1996)

Wet Autumn Night

Where are the firemen rushing in the rain?
Like a washed-up poet, will their siren blaze
capsize to damp fizzle? An Arab
fruit stand is backlit like Marlene Dietrich;
mango eyes follow us, as in a Renaissance
vanity. Ancient furies lean
on doorframes, hard as prostitutes,
their scarred mouths dubbed with fire-shrieks,
for they know that life, like rain,
evaporates. Down the cobbled street
ignore the stares from under canopies
of bars: umbrella envy—it too, shall pass.

STAINED GLASS AT PÈRE-LACHAISE

Earthly glory lasts, of course.
(Maps to celebrity graves, ten francs.) What passes,
caves in on the Age of Light: huts like toll booths
that split to bare an underworld
of cola bottles, cat food,
and stained glass, smashed by
this week's heathen at last week's
Kristallnacht. What's left
is magenta, sapphire, and opal.

Brown smoke, in a panic to escape
the crematorium, slaps the cold air,
clouding the glass, and tussles with the blue
before evanescing
into what we breathe.

Glass stays and goes, blitzkrieged
but intact across a century. Through gaps
in glass we see reality: glass is to be preferred—
Mary's come-hither look, Saint Gregory
thumbscrewing a book, a middle-class Parisian, his fat wife,
and a Saviour too soft to survive this life.

No Music

No music: the last of the house-rules
that a guest hears before cohabiting
the single-room flat on the superhighway:
no music, for one who spent months gone by
in fruitless debate on the greatness of Glenn Gould,
no requiems for those we may not love,
no music, but a hike to a suburban French
boneyard in summer, to pay our fresh respects to Satie,
A semiotic gravestone states that Monsieur Trou
—or Mister Hole— 80 years old, has found his hole
and lies there next to a butcher whose face on an inlaid
photo is a red capon crying as the abbatoir keens.
Here the wind is brainless and a pinkeyed bouquet
odalisques on a gravesite; soon it too will die.
Quiet. No music; no polkas, kazatskies or can-cans,
no mazurka, nocturne, or polonaise born
in the mind of Chopin, no *gymnopédie*, but
a new life commences, breathing, in silence and words.

LE BAR FLEURI

The only flower in sight is a hothouse orchid,
a fire extinguisher bleeding
on the wall; intaglioed
souvlakis weep by
the window, to be consumed
by the loveless and scorned.
Paris in winter:
should human affection show its face,
bottles of Pernod, Ricard, and Pastis
would stand on their heads in surprise.

Aquarium

The heat of naked spotlights and a waterfall's applause
do not trick three crocodile divas
into taking a bow. The hoary reptiles keep as still
as plates in an overpriced set of Buffon.
The aquarium air is damp and malodorous
as a summer lover's underarm;
Here too, the key is dominance:
two crocs colaborate to pin their lesser brother
under brackish water. Schoolkids, tasty morsels,
lean over iron bars (strictly forbidden)
and litter with money the animals' backs,
to whom it is no object, but a reflecting Fresnel
on their freeze-frame dance. To defy a future of handbags
and belts, the three green Graces open
their million-toothed jaws and roar.

SUMMER QUERIES AT THE MÉTRO SAINT-MICHEL

Why is Claude Lévi-Strauss,
"France's most influential intellectual,"
playing a rusty musical saw
before the Métro Saint-Michel?
Who taught him how, a Trobiand Islander
or Topa Inca Yupanqui?
The octogenarian *ethnologue*,
his spectacles misty and earlobes hairy,
makes Ming the Merciless noises,
cries from emotional fungus eaters
for a slew of doofus kids.
Japanese Elvis-impersonators do not even pause
to video, yet Swedes and Norwegians freeze.
Are they weirded out? "Man,
you wrote *Tristes Tropiques*," they do not say,
but lurch along their camelbackpack way.

AT THE JARDIN DES PLANTES ZOO

exhausted gorillas —CIORAN

Really, Koko darling, I am too pooped.
You seem a bit peaky as well.
Must be some primate form of Epstein-Barr's.
Every banana looks the same to me.
Even masturbating in the cage has palled
and that sure-fire stimulator,
the sight of Bomba's rose-red buttocks
(Time was, would start me off
fascinating kiddies and nuns)
has lost its *je-ne-sais-quoi.*
Let's face it, we're fatigued.
No longer ambitious enough to fart
brave melodies to rival IRCAM's,
we rest inert and only inadvertently
resemble orators of the right wing.
Perhaps our perpetual nudity has come to roost,
knowing we'll never need Balenciaga or Balmain.
My heavens, Bobo, even Saint-Laurent is but a name
to one who stays all day in the hairy rude.
How long since I've sidled to an animal lover,
accepted a coy peanut and pissed in his face?
Ah Jojo, the days that are no more!
Black Senegalese pass the cage
preoccupied with tourist sales.
I stare as if I'm sent to my reward
for years of service in the colonies.
Where's my pension, my tree-house, my little wife?
Koko, sing me a song of the dark rain forest;

At the Jardin des Plantes Zoo

Music might sweeten my plantain mash
served with an unspeakable house wine
that I've lost the desire to fling at humans.
Swinging from vine to vine has grown an idle chore.
Visiting hours at long last over,
When will come the African night?

PIGEONS IN THE MONTLHÉRY TOWER

Pigeons in the Montlhéry Tower
Hunch high atop the tourist trap,
trying to remember what they forgot,
Aging in winter above the raging threats
of car, cat, and plague. Pigeons in
the Montlhéry Tower, lacking
Stone Generals to decorate, build
Gaudí cathedrals of feather and dung
as companions. They have no truck
with avian coevals, rivals in
longevity. Ex-husbands and -wives
are cut, as in a novel by Ouida.
So high, what can one find
to eat but one's heart or carrion from a friend?
Outliving their generation, they glide
without a cluck or coo past medieval
floors, collapsed like failed marriages; pigeons
in the Montlhéry Tower, crust-eyed,
grey-white, prepare in silent triumph
to meet their god. Whatever
pigeon-purgatory may hold in store,
they know they have survived.

ICI MOURUT RACINE

Here died Racine: a sign
above the door of a square little cottage
made of feta cheese explains, and
the passerby's throat is a glottal stop
as forced as Bernhardt's *Phèdre*;
our feet are caught in time's caesura,
as alexandrines of life go on
behind lace curtains, people
eating baguettes and tripe and
who knows? writing five-act plays
and even the *clochard* in the littered street
proclaims, "Here died Racine,
but I'm alive!"

Perfect Weather in Clichy

Astral voyeur that I am,
to spy on a blue spring day
from behind the window, the sky frosted
with muck from a sleety life, is
better than a skittish hike
through a child-screaming park,
or dodging drivers' carbon-monoxide farts.
Edward Hopper might have traced
the solitary bee hunched in a wicker
chair, scribbling, and read as despair
the sane contentment of seeing Eden
without the pain of dwelling in the Promised Land.

CALL FOR BISHOP BERKELEY

Behind the frigorific Paris window,
steamed like the plate-glass of a brasserie's lobster tank,
Young Bacchus by Giambologna hot-plates morning coffee
through a bead curtain bespeaking Moroccan summer.
Bishop Berkeley, with his matchless gift
for positing unwitnessed deciduous falls,
might know the meaning of this morning beauty
straining at daybreak to start for the swimming pool,
unselfconscious as the Forest of Fontainbleau,
were no one present to savor him,
silent, sipping reheated
supermarket pseudo-brew.

EDVARD MUNCH TO HIS MUSE

Oslo's plenilune has a bad case of acne.
Tonight on the bridge, a medicinal smell.
I run like Napoleon, they still attack me,
but their cameras are useless in Heaven or Hell.

The man who resembles a London bobby
and his pal have passed, but their odor lingers.
They were waiting for us in the tenement lobby.
At the end of their hands, you can bet there'll be fingers.

Art critics have been diffusing their lies
since an awful disease with no Latin name
stank up their poetry and blinded their eyes.
One day soon their cufflinks shall burst into flame.

Then the night will be your sole redeemer,
the only sound, a switchblade's click.
And worry not, my precious Screamer —
the Man in the Moon has a dick.

TAPESTRY, MUSÉE MARMOTTAN

Death is pursuing the peasants.
A rustic old geezer high-tails it away,
hoisted by milkmaids who curdle in fright;
he was one of Breughel's gleaners till his kneecaps collapsed.

Death is coming on strong; its borzoi dogs
bite us with sting-ray eyes. The peasants flee
in the yellow night. The stitches in their sides
are sewn by near-sighted brides. The Battle
between Carnival and Lent is decided. Country faces
blacken to the colour of the tide; their
tapestry is short, and no place to hide.

Death is pursing the peasants,
its sickle is sharp as a heart attack.
A marathoner, Death breaks the
world record for the indoor drag, but
is never fazed by a steroid check. Blazoned
on fiber that buckles like a flag,
Mister *Timor Mortis*, Death, is back.

Cranach's
"Cupid as Honey Thief"

Staatsmuseum, Stuttgart

Put your hand in the honey-crack,
Amoretto. The tree has split
and inside a chubby paw slides.
Blind-side every bee
and immerse your pinky
in sticky sweet.

PERUGINO'S "SAINT JEROME SUPPORTING TWO HANGED YOUTHS"

Musée du Louvre

Leave home your lion, Jerome, and
lock up the Vulgate: nude boys
are hanging, and they are cute.
Stand between them, mighty as
Sarastro or Gertrude Stein,
and raise them above their nooses.
Jerry's kids, a saucy brunet
and Leonardo-curled blond,
stripped to a diaper, are displayed
like a brace of pheasants
in the *Grande Galérie*, saved
because a translator was near.

A *Trompe-l'Oeil* Portrait of the Poet, Cracow

Attention to your bones, Adam Mickiewicz,
who wrote *Pan Tadeusz* and scratched
through alleycat affairs
with whispering Marquesas
in the bibliothèque Mazarine.

Adam, here you lie:
a *trompe-l'oeil* painter froze you,
amid linen grey and convoluted like a brain.
Is this the palomino
that galloped across the Crimea's
boulders and waterfalls?
Now a glacier landscape awaits,
an infinity of ice, Lithuania in winter.

Epiphany at the Metropolitan Museum

In the B. Altman Galleries, an incomplete triptych:
gone is the centerpiece, Memling's Virgin and Child,
but the donors remain, a pair of lean Belgians
each in a frame, clasping their skinny hands
in less-intense-than-Dürer's prayer.
We also wait for something to happen,
a blessing or sign perhaps,
for a new-found friendship.
At once our faith's rewarded:
an unremarked door slides ajar, revealing
a den of grey security guards,
huddled as if for warmth
like winter pigeons in a cote.
Crammed within, they lounge, legs splayed,
with ponderous thighs against the wall,
round the boss's La-Z-Boy lounger.
Freed for the nonce from telling us the time
and where the toilets and Rembrandts are,
they are gentle, innocent, plump,
gaping like rustics at a nativity.
Above, on the dun-stained wall,
large Letraset letters proclaim,
GOD LOVES US ALL.
Oh yes, we both recall.

GERBRANDT VAN DER EECKHOUT'S "PORTRAIT OF HIS FATHER" (1650)

Musée de Grenoble

Being Gerbrandt and not
Rembrandt, I painted Papa's
senile humid eyes instead of my own,
in a plea-bargain to posterity.
I meant to illustrate a fly
or my mind, but a mystery
intervened: did my lack of narcissism
cost me immortality?
A riddle to unseat the
Polish Rider, that.
Our satin backdrops both melt
like brie, our ruffs are equally helical.
Dad's hands are gelid bijoux
up to the snuff of van Rijn.
You'd never see Gerbrandt making
his mom a sloppy Prophetess,
or Lut van der Eeckhout as a two-ton Danaë.
From my wall in Grenoble
I hear he didn't even paint his fame.
Who can disattribute a void?
Without a workshop scrumming,
my oblivion is mine.

PROLIFIC AFFECTIONS

In the art historian's study
on a bulletin board of brown cork
"It's Raining Men," as the disco song says—
dozens of postcards are pierced with tacks,
Old Master portraits of males that
she gathered from galleries here and abroad.
Men only are depicted,
their faces ascetic:
Van der Weyden's *Saint Ivo* stares hollow-cheeked
at Velasquez' slave, the only black.
The costumes, from codpiece to Renaissance drag
are bolder than in nearby Village bars.
The scholar pokes an IBM Selectric
as bought boys spy over her shoulders:
Botticelli's apprentices
who frame a tranquil tondo.
Her life is in these cards;
Assembled as a smiling wall of eros,
grouped closer than the retina
can seize them one by one,
they say she must always navigate
a hopscotch of passing desires.

THE BABY GRAND MACABRE

*His impediments grew upon him. He ran down after
going to bed, to make sure he had locked the piano;
he feared a burglar might wake him by playing it.*

—SANTAYANA, *The Middle Span*

Somewhere, I know, a pianist waits for me,
a man, a woman, or a four-handed team.
Inexorably, he (in speaking of tormentors, let's be
sexist) advances as a fiend in a dream.
Hands that mastered Mussorgsky must pick my lock,
penetrate my house, pass through my lobby,
and in the studio beneath an ormolu clock
he'll find my *Knabe.*
Inviolate, it stands on piano legs
black as the late Ferruccio Busoni's wigs.
The horror is not in the program he'll play,
whether Chopsticks or Czerny or Chabrier,
but that sure as insomnia, despite any pleas,
a marauder will tickle my ivories.
While I recline above in anxious wait,
probing fingers can caress my eighty-eight.
Bedded down with head under pillow,
I sense the following scenario:
My Maestro Anonimo, whom I cannot see,
lets out an arpeggio like an eruct at tea.
To realize all my anticipatory fits
he tears off Schumann's *Träumerei* like Horowitz.
I won't descend to play the solicitous host
when *Du Holde Kunst* trickles past my newel post
to where I lie, trying not to name that tune:
"Oh no, it can't be...Debussy's *Clair de Lune?*"

The Baby Grand Macabre

In a womanish voice I beg, "Oh please,
anything, Sir, but not Beethoven's *Für Elise*."
Sweat drenches my pyjamas, I can do no more,
but a plummy voice unknown to me sings out, "*Encore!*"

A Prayer Against Strauss' "Salomé," 1900

Sir Edward Elgar, so he told Frederick Delius,
was urged by New York's religious to pray
for the failure of Richard Strauss' new opera, "Salomé":

O Saint Cecilia, won't you intercede today
and stop this opera before it can blight us?
May its orchestra squint with conjunctivitis,
split lips afflict entire wind sections,
brass players be seized with random infections,
dropsies bloat the fiddlers' fingers,
and blessed Cecilia, as for the singers,
May the eponymous lead soprano,
who spouts so shamelessly Strauss' guano,
swell to bursting and grow a beard,
so the heathen present at the premiered
work mistake her for Wagner's late held-
entenor, Ludwig Schnorr von Carolsfeld.
Swathe the brazen hussy in reinforced concrete
and hang her over the Danube River by her feet
to waltzes by the *veritable* Strauss, Johann,
not this godless, uncivilized barbarian.

RIMBAUD'S PIANO

1875. Madame Rimbaud, bowing to
her son's pleas, rents a piano.

Madame erects a piano in the Alps,
hefted by Laurel and Hardy and
the absinthe ape. Madame tickles
the ivories, an epoch before it takes
Bach three compact discs to crucify
the Christ. Madame will Czerny
and Clementi all day long;
in Aden no ant-proof organ lies.
Madame boasts no Drunken Boat,
but an upright, varnished to hell,
will carry a load of foolscap
across a contraceptive mire.
Madame must caress them eighty-eight,
run guns, trade slaves, scream with gangrene,
say bye-bye. Critics of Symbolism,
"Al-Hamdo-lillah!"

FUNERAL MUSIC FOR CHRISTIAN DIOR

Black the trees on the Avenue Montaigne,
bending from noble, sandblasted stone.
Bare branches wave like paparazzi.
Black the bunting on the *premier étage*.
For Immediate Release: Dior has gone.
A gaggle of gorgeous mannequins
parades the Runway of the Dead,
towards the Montparnasse Cemetery.
Their shapely ankles cluster equidistantly,
a chain gang of allure.
Chic bracelets clink with every shuffle.
Each beauty, starved to a dark mist of anorexia,
bears an emblematic purse and pillbox hat,
and shrinks from fat Parisians who came to gawk.
Eighteen years before, shaved-headed *collaboratrices*
were quick-marched down an identical street,
trying to cradle Nazi-gendered newborn
spat at by some of the same *public*.
Today the crowd retains its saliva and sangfroid.
For Dior's staff, the sole conceivable shame
is in staying young and callipygean
after the patron has breathed his last.
But Yves Saint-Laurent is peering from the wings
as high heels beat a *marche-funèbre*
on the street of Montaigne, who should have called fashion
the art of learning how not to die.

TATYANA NIKOLAEVNA

San Francisco, November 24.
Russian pianist dies during concert.

Roll under the holy table,
Tatyana; Babushka went
pop at the piano.
Aneurysms roll like grapefruits
as crowds of San Franciscans face
a future of CD's, rigid
as guards at Lenin's Tomb.
"Tatyana's Letter" is sung by Ljuba Welitsch,
but what will you sing, tickler
of ivories? In a Russian accent, reply:
"No aneurysm. Like Russian dolls,
inside me was a small Tatyana,
inside another, down to the core,
all playing Préludes by Shostakovich—
it was she who burst, not me.
'Svedanya!"

Apology to Saint Cecilia

The shame of not being a musician.
— Cioran

Trace each bird's identity in the air
by Jacob van Ruysdael at the Kunsthalle,
Give time for poems, like sanctions, to work,
Still there's the shame
of not being a musician. All that is,
leans well or ill toward melody,
and we are merely scythes
smiling in a prepared Steinway.

Pray Cecilia, may we not aspire
to your toccatas, and fire off
the noonday martyrdom with
krumhorn, rebec, theorbo?
Sequester us from goats
who ogle unlined sheets
minus a *meno mosso!*

WHAT TIME DOES A CHINAMAN GO TO THE DENTIST?

The closest I've been or want to be to Beijing
is hard by these pristine drills, this spiral fountain
that asks the tourist not for yen, but spit.
Thank heaven for the curtains, smutty chintz
inherited from practices ago
and that confused supply room offstage right.
They make me less uptight;
To show a little dirt's Confucian.

"Your mouth is a camera," the Chinese dentist says.
I think of Auden's "Your mother's a camera,
Your mother's the Resurrection and the Life."
He adds, "You got teeth like my wife,"
maneuvering his quivering light
upon the film clenched in my calculus.

My X-rayed roots, a gothic deus,
grin insincerely as a skeleton
or Great Wall shutterbug's appalling "Cheese!"
"You open widely, please."
We've tacitly agreed:
He scrapes, I bleed.
The tiny tool works through until I'm spangled as a
        Gang War joss,
But Mott Street never tells you "Rinse" or "Floss."

CAPTIONS TO CERTAIN
SLIDE LECTURES

Opalakah, Michigan in haystack time
The rictus of Peloponnesian macrodents
All-American fullback Otiose Grimes
One moment after Walla Walla's history commenced
Angevine escutcheon with a *fleur-de-lis* above
A bust of Sartre made entirely of farina
The only man Aunt Lulu ever loved
An ex-Marine inside a manner of marina
The Bosnian widow's *a capella* choir on a walk
Silverlights of lesser auks
Why Titicaca never rivaled Teotihuacán
The bitter litter of Bellerophon.

FAILED CATHEDRALS

A bald architect friend speaks
of his joy in visiting failed cathedrals,
whose anonymous builders
in the Middle Ages royally fucked up
with naves that go nowhere, fallen
Gothic arches, off-color stained glass
that wouldn't pass at Disneyland.
Even inspired by eternity, these
humble craftsmen couldn't get it up.
Mary our Interceder may forgive most everything,
but not the Cathedral at Toulouse;
the French spent centuries and wound up
with an æsthetic zero. Failed cathedrals,
like brute colours by Dürer or a Mozart insipidity,
are not occasions to gloat, but solaces
for the banana peel concealed in every human
Vatican, where Laurel and Hardy, as papal nuncios,
proffer a jalopy bull.

A Lost Sugarcube
Will Pursue You in Hell

—Russian Proverb

A lost sugarcube will pursue you in hell,
shrieking the blood-red name of a bad hotel.
In its scorched wrapper, a cousin to the wife of Lot
looks back at caffeine inferno. Lost? Surely forgot,
but when and why? How many have I seen,
refined, unrefined, white, brown, and St. Patrick's Day green:
dental hitmen in square-shouldered suits,
unlike limp sacks of cancerous substitutes.
Now must I recall a sweet greed mislaid,
not crushed to coral in an amniotic cup;
around my spoon no colloid hurricane
to coat the torment of the tabletop.

CIORAN'S IDEAL CONFESSOR, JUDGMENT DAY

I dream of a blasé Saint.
—CIORAN

Order another novena as if from
a Club Med waiter,
kick me upstairs to heaven
for lack of the *je-ne-sais-quoi*
that might land me deep below,
Greet my nudest avowals
with an Adolphe Menjou yawn,
so I may personify
Eden's ennui, after
decades of interesting times.
I long for thee, blasé Saint,
displaying stigmata like Ray-Bans
on a California nose,
bearing as emblemata a microwave
and frequent flyer card,
machines of *your* martyrdom.
I straddle my herniated sins,
you know them all backwards:
"It's time for the Cosby Show
so *molto allegro*—
You think we have eternity
to waltz through your piddle?"

A sloppy cross chills the air
like graffiti on a manger,
the Pearly Gates bother to jostle ajar,
unshaven jaws barely separate,
and out slides the *Magnificat* of Bach.

Reading Proust in Barcelona

Growing organically, swelling and drying,
pressing forward, sticking great cucumbers
into the air, accumulating accretions,
the oyster's ulcer that becomes the pearl,
this is art by Antonio Gaudí,
whose snakes and salamanders climb
the sugared broccoli of the Sagrada Familia
Cathedral, whose towers can never be completed, any more
than they could be destroyed in Franco's war.
The gingerbread house that opens a fairyland park
is boarded up, the witch is gone, and the
sugar-glaze chipped and nibbled by mice.
Carry Proust's novel through the streets of Barcelona,
hold it breast-high like Moses bearing the law,
a Giotto emblem, or calling card, like the gold pince-nez
outside the optometrist's plate-glass, a gigantism as useless
as works by Proust or Gaudí, but representing what we
aspire to. Marcel's book is childhood
like chocolate Gaudí drank at teatime instead of tea.
Show Proust to the Gaudí towers
who see it all, exactly like a rhododendron
that grows more zestfully if loving words
are murmured in its ear. Show them the Proust as a relief
from sightseeing busloads and they will recognize a friend
and wave their knobby warts in the dusty breeze.

Birthplace of Colette

Yonne is the name of the land
where she was born.
Farms and cows abound.
In the central butcher shop are found
pigsfeet: frozen, huge and dead,
garnished with sprigs of parsley.

When the townsfolk once heard it said
that old frizzy-hair in a wheelchair
wished to visit, they nearly had a lynching.
What —after her years of dancing
undressed with transvestite ladies?

Now she's dead, which makes a difference,
so tourist signs welcome
all with dollars, marks, and yen.
The newsstand stocks her novels,
stacked beside the porno
where they cast a feline eye
at profiteering on the hated dead,
a local rite
since long before the German Occupation.
God what has become of this nation?

POETRY OF EXILE:
ZAGAJEWSKI AND BRODSKY

A gleaming head perfectly bald,
Legs planted firmly in Oxford bags
upon a stage set who knows why
in red crêpe as a Wild West bar,
complete with booze. The poet drinks plain water.
Stage right, a horse pried from a carousel,
eyes big in fear or pain.
A golden pole bisects its backbone
like Cocteau stabbed by a funhouse pen.

Our first man of the evening, Adam,
like his namesake creates new words:
dan-*dell*-ion, tuxeddo, pe-O-nies,
each shocks the ear with pleasure,
bionets for bayonets, Caesars for scissors,
ounce for aunts.
The merry-go-round beast winces
but keeps its best foot forward.
"Dance mist" the poet says, for dense.
Red, blue, and fuchsia ribbons flutter from the flies.

Then Brodsky, whose stutters are enlaurelled by the Muse:
"The uh-uh-uh, the uh-uh-uh, the title-uh-uh-uh,"
He dedicates a poem to the reader who preceded him,
then gulps a mouthful from the glass that Adam left,
unconscious act of body solidarity.
His prideful posture scolds the milkman
for bringing too much cream.
Harried words are spit out like cab directions:

"Wild mayors carousing," no, mares.
A verse in honor of Miss Susan Sontag
"Who's in the audience, I trust."
A Prince Valiant haircut bobs from the front row.

Brodsky holds his ear like Ella singing scat
to shut out poison imps of English,
"the language of the evening,"
explained with no small scorn.
And sure enough, the demons win.
Something is "on the key," no, no.
He looks into the silent void. "Where, where is Susan?
How do you spell embankment, key kway?"
He means how to pronounce a quay.
Sontag and others murmur it, the spell is broken,
but exile again untunes the poet's "grand piana."

Ten Lines Before the Mast

The Indian Ocean's verdant ichor
flows past the four-master's rusty anchor;
The Second Mate and Captain bicker
over a bosun they happen to hanker
after. No Yale College, no more a banker,
on the whale's back I breathe the salty liquor.
Lord Jim, *Narcissus* senza *Nigger*,
I feel as if I'd witnessed Angkor
Wat or Borobodur; my biceps grow thicker
and on my bonny lip, is that a chancre?

A Friend of Larkin's

Groping back home after a proper bash at four,
I looked up from the cobbled street. A square of light
shone out, curtains parted by an old bore.

The turkey-wattled baldy looked into the night.
I knew that Thatcher-lover all right;
I'd seen him on telly before.

Deaf-aid in his ear, scouring the street
for sexy young kids or unemployeds,
gloating in envy at every bloke he'd meet.

You'd think he never quite enjoyed
a love-life on his own. He had no pride,
the way he'd simper at me and Marguerite

As if he'd like to watch us fuck.
He writes. I said, "Books are a load of crap."
The poor gob's eyes lit up behind his specs.

Even for Hull, the boy's a bally sap.
God only knows what caught him in this trap.
God pity the sad, solitary bugger's luck.

From a Memoir of Auden

He would cry out, "Here's Mom!" when we
entered the Holland Tunnel.
—V. Yanovsky.

The Poet is crying out, "Here's Mom!"
On entering the Holland Tunnel.
"Here's Pop!" is saved for the Empire State
Building, while Auntie Grace
is every inch Grant's Tomb.
Any fool can see Uncle Harry in
the Verrazano Narrows Bridge
while much of Cousin Sandy remains,
alas, pure Spuyten Duyvel.
Some nephews are no more than the Fraunces Tavern,
Brother Bob the Bowne House,
and of the sisters, Jane may stay Jumel Terrace,
But Alice shall always be the Palisades.

At the Bibliothèque

Typical scene in the
Central Library, Jamaica, Queens:

A large black woman in her Sunday best,
white lace in her hair,
marches past the biographies,
proclaiming to all and sundry:

"I tell you about a science book—
Experiment on an egg with your eyes.
Experiment in the *lavat'ry*
on an egg with your eyes."

LIGHTNING MAY STRIKE

A boutique sells *"Farces et Attrapes"*
across the street, but here the sagging
party masks can't be removed.
In a continuity of drool, a crone takes my arm:
"Young man, you are on the Grand Tour?"
Yes, but where are Rousseau and Voltaire?
In the hallway, electrical closets
bear a bee-yellow warning—
a silhouetted man is falling, fired
by bolts of lightning. Death froze
the chump in a charleston,
exacto elbows held high.
How quick! How painless!
Less fortunate voices cry out tunes
in the rec room, muzak for
an odd-smelling Otis.
Old Pandora leads me to
the lift. We wait in silence for the box's
doors to swing ajar.

Nursing Home

Where human silhouettes
reduce to signposts for the toilet,
and ancient spouses reunite for trysts
with warty deathmasks of the Abbé Liszt,
we wait. Time drips like spittle,
in no rush to traverse a famous face,
that plays the game of change-the-word:
hospital, hotspur, horsepiss, hospice.

LONGEVITY

Each night when the TV news is bad,
the octogenarian watch goes into effect:
by common consent the old sit slack-jawed, sunken-eyed,
before their sets, agreeing not to sleep,
tormented by the images producers keep using,
of soccer fans trampled to death
or three-year-olds strangled and raped.
They sit alone crying; even the psoriatic dog
by the fire has long ceased to lick his privates
and fitfully snores, dreaming of skin that is smooth.
The old ones think of a backyard in the country
once tomato-ripe; now the vines
are flat and brown as squashed sports lovers
and the plot is coffin-shaped, like the future.
While the rest of the nation catches its beauty rest,
the octogenarians are outraged to the core
by what man does to man.
Their meditation through the night is not a prayer
but a contemplation of the empty tube
that stays when the picture fades,
true vacancy, the vacuum faced
by the octogenarian watch that goes into effect
each night when the TV news is bad.

OLD TENANTS

In our co-op apartment, others have died.
Do doormen cry, staring at the intaglio,
when ambulances, like dachshunds, come and go?
In our apartment, like Lady Macbeth,
the fact of death hovers, frets, and mutters:
Home is the place you die, but
an apartment belongs to others.
By and by, their profiles emerge:
"Oh Mister and Missus Zip, they whined about the noise
and chill, their dog was ill, they never tipped."
Shadows of a former frigidaire
whiten the wall, as we peer in the mirror
to prove we're not "unknown at this address."
Plastic stickers on the shower floor, left over
from an age of faith, say, "If I place
ugly green daisies in my tub, I will not fall
and break my bones and go to a home." They got
their wish, so why the closeted reproach
of moldy books by Mazo de la Roche?

Turning Point in Barcelona

The idea that sleep is the sweetest benefice
is disproved by the beloved one's
nap in the Parc de la Ciutadella.
Particoloured lights, three old *señoras* arm-in-arm,
a cyclist's thighs —all are missed
by the one who feels absence of pain is the thing.
Lying shrivelled like a Civil War cadet
changed by a bullet into a mess of clothes,
he cannot see that the park is beautiful, people are passing,
and we ourselves might be beautiful,
so I tell it to the pungent wrapper
of a *bocadillo* sandwich.

SHORTS

AUTHOR PORTRAIT

Greasy meaty face
held up by hotdog fingers:
Karsh's Graham Greene.

TANKA: DISTRACTIONS OF A
TRAVELLING SHOT

Café cinema—
Gramps snatches Sonny's cola;
punk lovers bicker.
Bloop! I go down the métro
steps, somehow feeling better.

SKYSCRAPER DISSUASION

Wavering on a ledge,
your life choked with bile,
Never drop off the edge—
Enemies would smile!

Three A.M.

Exhale, swimmer,
create a breeze between my eyebrows
from lungs that drummed
salt from Brazilian seas.
Exhale upon me
mouth to mouth now,
you asleep, I not,
so that my eyebrows
feed and aggrandize
like those of John L. Lewis, Czeslaw
Milosz or Oscar Homolka,
breathe out the breeze of sambas
by Gilberto Gil and Djavan,
breathe freely, with force and *fervor*.
Begin a wind tunnel that
vacuums my heart, till
I search for a poem
and you've turned to the wall, statue-still.

Sonnet to Sabu

Ya' Rasullalah! I want to be a jar
(How many did we buy at *Jai Hind* stores?)
of Indian chewing betel, *Pan Bahar*.
By night I'd idly slip into your pores,
transpiring as persimmon Paki sweat,
a sweeter scent than Saint-Laurent can sell.

Under your catpink, muscled tongue I'd swell,
past teeth brown as a memsahib's barrette.
Your molars and incisors do me in,
pulverizing all to a chewy paste.
You swallow, sated, give your catfish grin,
and take more stimulating me to taste.

But stoutly would I suffer such disaster,
Knowing each bit of Ben beats your heart faster.

FÊTE NATIONALE

The night is long
Without any dream;
Draped statues,
Crisp like crinoline,
Dissolve in flame.
"You are not *beau*,
but I desire you
because of your mind,"
I am told, which harkens to a day
company may be paid for.
Eyes closed, the shade we see
is conservatory green:
Like miserable street mimes
we see who budges first—
dry box-spring cadenzas
tell me I'm not alone.

OVA IN THE KITCHENETTE

The Royal Assassination Squad arrived
while your personal soft-boiled egg was sitting,
paring its toenails before the electric fire,
listening to a broadcast of the Mormon Salmonella Choir.
At breakfast, you tapped the membrane,
scarcely expecting a rap in reply.
No omelette is made by breaking my eggs, dear heart,
nor my thin shell of kitchen sensation.
Of course you may leave at will, but please "go quiet,"
recalling my date of expiration.
Decapitate this egghead to yellow gore,
the stuff they root for in right-to-life films;
Your critique of how to boil a three-minute-wonder
leaves me cold, I might add —would you prefer
a morning Fabergé prepared
for hemophiliac Czars, in blue diamonds and fox-furs,
a cholesterol Liberace?

Just Say No

A night of cocaine and *Bajazet* by Jean Racine:
Malraux's white tabby cat
climbs his tuxedoed back
after a final violin recital,
gloved fingers executing the *Chaconne* of Bach
while funhouse mirrors out of eyeshot
wheel into the wings.
Tonight a Walkman should be worn
to delimit the boundaries of the brain.
A sofa green as me becomes
a Paris park with unpaved ways,
where pigeon droppings besiege the brow
of a poor bust of Baudelaire.
A horse jogs by, allowing us to ogle
his sweat-stained, muscled coat.
There are too many flowers here to pick
and the pasture is limitless,
a glacier melts behind the nose
as an Ice Age reaches the teeth.
In the bathtub, genitals float like Ophelia.
Soapy Ophelia, your sex excites no more,
not even as a sonnet's theme:
Glimpse the coming attractions of impotence,
no longer stage-struck for a prick.
Who set the *Discobolos* on my knees?
Each inhalation brings nostalgia to the nose
until the sound-and-light show shuts
abruptly as video-porn,
a vanishing box declines
to integral calculus, encasing the skull
in hot aluminum bricks.

MUSÉE DES BEAUX ARTS, 1989

In a room next to Auden's favorite pic,
our mirror today is Bartholomew's Martyrdom,
by a minor Spanish master.
The flayer holds a dripping knife
between his teeth to better strip
the epidermis. What else is new?
We circle back to barbarity
with the drift of museum closing time.
Chocolate munchers cram the corporate-sponsored
show, grossing out on Gothic pain,
Gallery guards are shockproof in uniformed hells,
living with static horrors ever in view.
A step away, Breughel's Icarus is melted down
by the party in power. Instead of
drowning, he grows old and phthisic
in an isolation cell. His wife campaigns for amnesty.
Not a prayer. Dædelus is creamed by a buzzbomb,
in a café beside four Catholic nuns.
Life can't go on after Treblinka and Vietnam,
Our god is Walter Cronkite and boy, is he pissed,
and no horse has an innocent behind.

WHAT THE CHURCH DOME TELLS US

Baldacchinos no better than Bernini's
spiral upwards in a Paris church
that missed the boat for baroque.
Frescoed martyrs by minor masters
are splayed across the dome. Saints hand over
their guts or hang upside down
like Commie cosmonauts. Their pain is
silent, except for a moan
from the oppressive dome—
Who voiced a miracle?
Just a pigeon that transgressed
a stained-glass window
and wildly keens that our life
must be delimited by a dome.
Human forms, at equidistant
shrines, don't even lift their eyes.

Two Couplets

Expectancy

Asthmatic, myopic, at thirty-eight worried:
At this age, my betters have often been buried.

Meditation at a Bar

Think long and hard on the words of the Yoruba wise-
man: "Overhandsome people are skeletons in disguise."

HUMMINGBIRD LESSONS

For three minutes, free
from the weight of mental
cruelty, on this balcony
I watch the matinal
activity of insect, bird, and neighbour.
The latter offer facetious talk
about fæces—how superior
is the breakfast of the birds:

The misnamed hummingbird
does not hum, but thrums,
a raccoon's belch in the air,
flashing a turquoise underbelly
where sugar-water sits,

A fencing match, where beaks
insert at the killing point
of a garish feeder.
Stagnant yellow water
is ambrosia to he who slides,
turns and rolls. Who is he avoiding
by these fighter-pilot formations?

What *Guns of Navarone* scenario
is flashing through your brain
as you slant, glide, feint,
to sip in a plastic daisy?

Hummingbird Lessons

Why expend tons of energy
and Balanchine choreography
against assailants
who don't exist?
Your negative example teaches us:
where water is plentiful,
go right up and drink.

The Bay of Rio

With fractal inevitability,
the Sugar Loaf Mountain
and the *favelas*
say, "So must we be."

Cumulous outlines
barely hide truth
draped in Mythology.
Two hungry dogs,
a mother and child,
lust after cold coconut water
and frying meat.

We cannot stop
along the suicidal highway.
Brothers of Brazil,
who ironize our sweat
while discouraging the flies—
I have known heat like this
in New York City.

Outside the car window,
an emaciated woman
beats the mother dog.
Icosahedrons of oranges
dangle by the road,
prey to every breeze,
as poor folk tout their wares
to the rich in limousines,
in a land where everything
seems to have a meaning.

Seen in the Sky From a Train
Near Compiègne

Cloud lovelies over Noyon—
Legs and torsos truncated,
not by serial murder, but shaded
with skill in cumulus grey.
Monet's haystacks claim,
"Of no importance is the sky,
mere slabs of white hovering
beside blue hay, blue soil."
But over Noyon are
cloud pterodactyls,
the coupling of Roman gods,
and Moby Dick handing
a marathoner's baton
to the Decalogue.
O tablets of the Lord, what
are you forbidding in the sky?

Netsuke People

Musée d'Ennery, Paris

Netsuke people, as artists,
are crushed by the weight of the real estate
on the avenue Foch, where Maria Callas shrieked her last.
Poor as the poet "disguised as a beggaress,"
Netsuke people have economic flaws:
their cheap loincloths are caught in the jaws of a clam.
They put a hard-boiled egg to their eyes
instead of glasses. The only fun they can afford
is to laugh beside a giant's severed member.

Netsuke people know that the seven
sages in a wood of bamboo are blocked from view
by tourists in floor-length mink.
A God of Longevity dictating to a Boy-Scribe,
docks his ship behind chalcedony spires.

The rich come visiting from every land but Japan, where
nobody gives a hoot about netsuke. This they realize,
netsuke people, and squeeze their emigré ears
and cry a multiple-lacquered cry.

EMIGRÉ PARTY

Landscapes of Split and Bled appear behind
football-shaped heads, partygoers ripe for
jokes and bad songs from the sixties.
Obeisance to a *blini* precedes
the oath to state-approved *hors d'oeuvres*.
Espionage catches a cuckold only too ready
to display his pectorals, while exiles wear the biretta
of Cardinal Mindszenty.
Some guests vanish early, after a secret trial,
and everyone feels about his home like Chekhov's wife:
a bitch, and distant, but somehow beloved,
though "their marriage was not a happy one."
Masha in black no longer yearns for Moscow,
the Olga Knipper of our exiles' dreams.

LOVE'S SIGNATURE

Scouting Paris like a dumdum bullet
seeking a place to implode, I look down at the
Boulevard de Montparnasse, where a
love-besotted Frenchman has
tried to write his girlfriend's name
upon the sidewalk in piss. Cursive
letters spell out the sacred appellation:
A N N E - M A R I— he almost made it.
Couldn't he find another uroscript
to lend a friendly helping prick?
The morning after, people hurry past, not reading
the acid imprint that the dew didn't
fade. They may attribute the blots to
a bison-bladdered Alsatian bitch,
but how might Anne-Marie reply, whose name
a lover penned corrosively
for all the French to see
in pee?

MARIE COUGHING

Queen Lear goes Howl, Howl, Howl,
If you be men, where are your stones?
Marie, gag reflexes agly,
chokes on particles of Keats in the air,
an arrow in her quiver
of reaction: give her a glass of booze
and she'll throw a narcoleptic trance
to teach the children how to dance;
Possessing coughness or sleep, means
she and the cough and sleep are one.
Rattling the shafters,
Straddling the poofters,
Crafty for readers,
Marie is our cougher laureate,
for better it is, she knows, to be
cougher than coffin'd
or coffee-mate.
Dick Nixon couldn't get it down Pat,
what Marie can't get down
is the poetry critic who looks like
John Sununu in drag,
or that we all are prison-poets
in manacles not only from our minds
but real and steel and framed
by other's hands. When the gates
are slammed on money, work, and sex,
to solitude and pity, they
open again at a cough from Marie,
the bronchial sesame that
signals our hearts' combustion.

She drapes her face in embroidered lace
like a Shulamite veiling her mysteries,
the *chadur* for a harem of mind—
Marie, in your seminar at the
Y, cough!

SAINT JOHN NAP

Drowsing to a Bach oratorio on the radio set,
hanging front-to-back in a seriously unmade bed,
bloated by a brunch of loaf and rillettes,
we twine like thieves crucified,
to save crosses, on a single tree.
Having thrice denied each other,
we succumb to killer gravity,
our physiques more slack
than aerobic Saviours directed by Scorcese.
The heat, not light, we generate in tons
makes tastebuds fill with vinegar sips
from sponges of Centurions.
Your sharpened thumbnail serves
as crown of thorns to my right ear.
Heathen jeer each shift of thigh
that joins our bodies, and cry:
"See how his bloody back is just like the sky!"

Paradise for the Portuguese Queen

The Queen of Portugal has gone mad. Her mad-
ness consists of thinking herself in heaven. But
heaven is below what she expected. She
wanders around muttering, "Hmph!"
—— Hugo, *Choses Vues.*

Who has seen the sunflower has seen the sun,
says Camoens in *The Lusiades*, but I hardly
expected to see my duenna and her hairy mole,
nor my maidservant dwarf, malodorous
as ever, nor my already-bearded Infante, not now,
not *here*. Had I only known that life is a sphere
of reality beyond which nothing lies...*hmph!*
But holy Peter and his clichéd key
are just toys for the pinhata. I can see there's
no Gate and no up, down, or Purgatory,
no seraphim with polychromed wings
like the ornithologically exact Van Eyck
that still hangs in my toilet,
Heaven to the smallest feather—
No, I cannot bear this Paradise,
but to abdicate? *Hmph!* Speaking biblically,
only two upstarts have been to Eden and back,
their names Eve and Adam. Oh yes,
I forgot —and the snake. And the third
to escape was the snake.

ABOUT THE AUTHOR

BENJAMIN IVRY, after a long stint as a Paris-based cultural corre-
spondent, returned to America in 1996. His poems have appeared
in *The New Yorker*, *The New Republic*, *The London Review
of Books*, *The Spectator*, *Ambit*, and many other magazines.
His poetry translations from the Polish, *Canvas*, in colla-
boration with Renata Gorczynski, were published by
Farrar/Straus/Giroux in New York and Faber &
Faber in London. He has published biogra-
phies of Francis Poulenc (Phaidon) &
Maurice Ravel (Everyman/Knopf).
He also translates from the
French (*Albert Camus:
a Life* for Knopf)
& lectures on
the arts.
This is his first collection of poems.